South Africa

Tradition, Culture, and Daily Life

MAJOR NATIONS IN A GLOBAL WORLD

Books in the Series

South Africa

Tradition, Culture, and Daily Life

MAJOR NATIONS IN A GLOBAL WORLD

John Perritano

Mason Crest

Mason Crest
450 Parkway Drive, Suite D
Broomall, PA 19008
www.masoncrest.com

Printed and bound in the United States of America.

First printing
9 8 7 6 5 4 3 2 1

Series ISBN: 978-1-4222-3339-9
ISBN: 978-1-4222-3350-4
ebook ISBN: 978-1-4222-8590-9

The Library of Congress has cataloged the hardcopy format(s) as follows:

Library of Congress Cataloging-in-Publication Data

Perritano, John.
  South Africa / By John Perritano.
     pages cm. -- (Major nations in a global world)
  Includes index.
  ISBN 978-1-4222-3350-4 (hardback) -- ISBN 978-1-4222-3339-9 (series) -- ISBN 978-1-4222-8590-9 (ebook)
  1. South Africa--Description and travel--Juvenile literature. I. Title. II. Series: Major nations in a global world.
  DT1719P47 2015
  968--dc23

                         2015005033

Developed and produced by MTM Publishing, Inc.
        Project Director   Valerie Tomaselli
        Copyeditor   Lee Motteler/Geomap Corp.
        Editorial Coordinator Andrea St. Aubin

Indexing Services   Andrea Baron, Shearwater Indexing

Art direction and design by Sherry Williams, Oxygen Design Group

Contents

KEY ICONS TO LOOK FOR:

 Words to Understand: These words with their easy-to-understand definitions will increase the reader's understanding of the text, while building vocabulary skills.

 Sidebars: This boxed material within the main text allows readers to build knowledge, gain insights, explore possibilities, and broaden their perspectives by weaving together additional information to provide realistic and holistic perspectives.

 Research Projects: Readers are pointed toward areas of further inquiry connected to each chapter. Suggestions are provided for projects that encourage deeper research and analysis.

 Text-Dependent Questions: These questions send the reader back to the text for more careful attention to the evidence presented there.

 Series Glossary of Key Terms: This back-of-the book glossary contains terminology used throughout this series. Words found here increase the reader's ability to read and comprehend higher-level books and articles in this field.

Scenic view of the Blyde River Canyon,
South Africa.

INTRODUCTION

Located at the southern tip of Africa where the Atlantic and Indian Oceans meet, South Africa is a land of immense beauty and vast wealth, a country that is slowly recovering from the deep racial divisions that marred its history. Nearly as large as Great Britain, France, and Sweden combined, South Africa is one of the richest, largest, and the most industrialized country in Africa. Its climate is extremely dry in some areas, while other areas experience tremendous rainfall. It has a mountainous coastline, gleaming cities, and poverty-stricken slums.

Nearly 80 percent of the country's population are black and 9 percent are white. Until the late twentieth century, the white minority ruled the country's political and social landscape with a heavy racist hand, instituting a policy of apartheid that created untold economic, social, and cultural hardships for blacks. That all began to change in the 1980s as the country began to fully democratize. Today, at least on paper, South Africa is one nation no longer divided by race, although social, economic problems persist, and inequality still runs rampant. Yet, South Africans relish the idea of being a "rainbow nation."

"At home in South Africa I have sometimes said in big meetings where you have black and white together: 'Raise your hands!'" Bishop Desmond Tutu, a social-rights activist once said. "Then I have said: 'Move your hands,' and I've said 'Look at your hands—different colors representing different people. You are the Rainbow People of God.'"

Nelson Mandela led the anti-apartheid movement in South Africa and became the country's first black president.

WORDS TO UNDERSTAND

commonwealth: an association of sovereign nations unified by common cultural, political, and economic interests and traits.

conspiracy: secret dealings of a group of people aimed at accomplishing an illegal act.

Napoleonic: pertaining to French emperor Napoleon Bonaparte.

sabotage: destructive activity aimed at weakening a business or government.

CHAPTER ①

History, Religion, and Tradition

On May 10, 1994, *the New York Times* announced that South Africa had undergone a seismic shift in its history.

> Cape Town, South Africa. "The power that had belonged to whites since they first settled on this cape 342 years ago passed today to a Parliament as diverse as any in the world, a cast of proud survivors who began their work by electing Nelson Mandela to be the first black president of South Africa."

For the first time in its long history, South Africa's majority population was in control and democracy was beginning to bloom.

Nelson Mandela casts his vote in the 1994 presidential election, which he won; it was the first time he had ever voted.

MANDELA ON TRIAL

Nelson Mandela was the face of the anti-apartheid movement. At his trial for **sabotage** and **conspiracy**, he said violence was necessary if South Africa was to change. "South Africa belongs to all the people who live in it," he said. "It's an ideal for which I am prepared to die."

Prior to the election, South Africa had denied blacks the most basic human rights. Because of their skin color, South Africa's black majority could not live or work where they wanted. They were told where to go to school and what subjects to study. They were beaten and killed and thrown in prison. They could not mingle with whites and lived in outrageous slums.

Pictured here are indigenous people of southern Africa whose territory spans a wide region, including that of South Africa and neighboring countries.

This painting by Charles Davidson Bell (1813–1882) shows the arrival of Dutch settlers in South Africa in 1652.

Interestingly, the first inhabitants of South Africa, the San and Khoekhoe people, lived in relative harmony. The San, who lived in South Africa for nearly 30,000 years, still inhabit their ancestral lands, as do the Khoekhoe, who have been around for 2,000 years. Both groups were hunters and gatherers who led a nomadic lifestyle.

The first European to set eyes on South Africa was the Portuguese navigator and sailor Bartholomeu Dias. In February 1488, Dias spotted the southernmost point of Africa, the present-day Cape of Needles. Dias' eyes then gazed on a rocky second cape, which he named the Cape of Storms, later known as the Cape of Good Hope.

The colonial oppression of South Africa began soon after the first Europeans arrived. In 1652, the Dutch East India Company founded the first European settlement on the Cape, one that could provide ships traveling to the East Indies with much-needed supplies. Dutch settlers moved to the area where they found the San and Khoekhoe.

As the numbers of Dutch settlers increased, they moved slowly inland and colonized new areas for their farms and ranches. They pushed the local Africans out of their homes, taking many as slaves. Most of the Dutch men who arrived in South Africa did not come with wives. Instead, they sought out local women, which resulted in a mixed race of children known as Coloureds. The Coloureds are still considered a distinct race in South Africa.

This painting by Charles Davidson Bell (1813–1882) depicts the Zulu attack on a Boer camp in 1838.

Conflict was inevitable. The Dutch periodically fought the new local natives they encountered, including Zulus, one of the Bantu-speaking tribes that dominated the area. Meanwhile, Huguenots (French Protestants persecuted in France), along with German settlers, traveled to Cape Town and began to settle the region.

By the end of the **Napoleonic** Wars in 1815, the British displaced the Dutch as a tsunami of English settlers flocked to the tip of Africa. The Dutch colonists, known as Boers (the Dutch word for "farmer"), resented the British, refusing to live by their rules. By this time, the Dutch had developed a culture of their own, including a language called Afrikaans, a version of Dutch and German spoken by masters and slaves.

Instead of falling under the yoke of the much-despised British, the Boers moved further northward—a journey they called the Great Trek. About 12,000 Afrikaner farmers made the trip, establishing settlements in the middle of black South Africa in what would later become the Transvaal and the Orange Free State. The Trekkers believed they were moving onto vacant, unused land, an opinion not shared by the local Zulus and other native tribes.

Then in 1867, a discovery—diamonds—was made in the Orange Free State that would shape South Africa's destiny. Soon after, gold was discovered in Transvaal. The British and Boers vied for control of these wealthy areas.

The British had the upper hand and took over the diamond and gold mines. A few speculators became very rich and turned hundreds of thousands of natives into migrant workers.

Digging for diamonds at Kimberley-Kopje in 1872, drawn by J. Vanione in 1881.

The British also pushed the Africans who lived near the mineral deposits off their land. Subjugating a native population was common practice for the British. They had done it in other regions with much success. The Boers were a different problem. Like the British, they were white, European, and educated in Western culture. Still, in the minds of the British, they needed to be brought into line.

CONFLICT AND IMPRISONMENT

The British imprisoned 116,000 Afrikaner women and children in concentration camps during the Boer War. In addition, the British forced 115,000 Africans into these prisons. Disease and starvation killed about 42,000 whites and blacks in the camps.

In 1899, the Boers, led by Paul Kruger, president of the Transvaal, declared war on the English. The war did not end well for the Boers, whom the English handily defeated two years later. Black Africans used the conflict to reclaim some of their land, a move that was short lived. After the defeat, in 1910, both the English and the Boers created the Union of South Africa, a self-governing colony in the British **Commonwealth**.

The political and economic suppression of South Africa's blacks began in earnest. The new government did not give blacks full citizenship or the right to vote. Feeling politically isolated, they formed the African National Congress (ANC) in 1912. The following year, the division between white and black was made more pronounced with the passage of the Natives Land Act. The law divided the new nation into "white" and "black" areas. Through the Native

An anti-apartheid protest that took place at the South Africa House in London in 1989.

(Urban Areas) Act of 1923, the cities were reserved for "whites" and off limits to blacks who did not have jobs there. The townships outside city limits were "black." By 1936, whites controlled 87 percent of the land, while the black majority controlled 13 percent of the worst acreage in the country.

STUDENT PROTESTS

In 1976, black students revolted in the township of Soweto, near Johannesburg, on June 16, when the government insisted they learn Afrikaans, the language of the white minority. The army fired on the protesters, killing a 13-year-old boy named Hector Pietersen. The protests later spread from town to town killing nearly 600 people.

By the middle of the twentieth century, the government had enacted a new set of laws under the umbrella of apartheid. Apartheid segregated the races even further. It outlined where blacks could and could not live. It specified which schools they could attend and which jobs they could work. The government forced blacks to carry passes that proved they had jobs.

The system of apartheid became more entrenched as the years wore on. The government created ten "homelands" where blacks had to stay if they were not working for white employers. Eventually, South Africa's black population rose up, tossing South Africa into one bloody crisis after another. Finally, after years of international pressure, apartheid ended and a new era for South Africa dawned with the election of Nelson Mandela as the country's first black president.

TEXT-DEPENDENT QUESTIONS

1. Explain the causes of the Boer War.

2. Explain how the system of apartheid kept blacks and whites separated.

3. When did Nelson Mandela become president of South Africa?

RESEARCH PROJECTS

1. Use the Internet and the library to research more about apartheid and America's "Jim Crow" laws. Create a chart comparing and contrasting the two. What are the similarities? What are the differences? How did each government react?

2. Research and create a photo collage of the South African struggle against apartheid. For each photo you find, write a caption describing what is happening in the photo.

A few huts from a traditional Ndebele village in South Africa.

Family members gather outside a church in South Africa.

WORDS TO UNDERSTAND

ancestral: relating to ancestors or relatives who have lived in the past.

interpersonal: relating to the relationships or communication between people.

patrilineal: relating to the relationship based on the father or the descendants through the male line.

polygamy: the practice of having more than one spouse.

CHAPTER 2

Family and Friends

South Africa likes to call itself the "rainbow nation," a country made up of varying cultures, people, traditions, and languages. At the heart of this melting pot is the family, which means different things to different people. While the country's political struggles are over, the relationships between people of different races still smack of the racial and economic divisions that marred the country's history.

In some South African communities, the nuclear family—parents living with children and working together as a unit—dominates; while in other communities the focus is on the extended family, where more than one generation lives under the same roof.

A Zulu village near Durban, on South Africa's eastern coast.

South Africa's population is roughly 50.6 million people. Of that number, 80 percent are black African, of which 9 million are Zulu. As with other traditional African cultures, Zulu society is built around the family. The Zulus believe that every member is obligated to work for the betterment of family. When a baby is born, the entire village helps raise the child.

The Zulus practice both monogamy and **polygamy**. Polygamy was common in Zulu tribes until the nineteenth century, when white European missionaries began preaching Christianity and forced Zulu men who wanted to convert to divorce their "extra" wives.

In rural areas today, polygamy is still a natural part of life, while Zulu men living in the city tend to have only one wife. For Zulu polygamists, having more than one wife not only improves the family's social status but also adds extra income.

The Zulus are a **patrilineal** society, which means that kinship ties, such as inheritance, are passed through father's side of the family. The man is not only the head of the household but also the central figure of authority. In a patrilineal culture such as the Zulu's, the women are responsible for cooking, cleaning, and other household chores. They are also responsible for rearing the children. Many Zulu households have several generations, including grandparents and uncles living under one roof.

Just as family plays an important role in Zulu society, so do tribes. In such traditional African cultures, the tribe, whose clans, or family groups, live in defined territories and often share **ancestral** links, provides emotional and financial security. The chief, who speaks for his people, is the head of the tribe. The Zulu, like many traditional Africans, believe their ancestral spirits are a guiding force in their lives. They make offerings and sacrifices to them, believing these ancestral spirits will provide a bountiful harvest, good health, and the prosperity of the village.

NATURAL HEALING

Traditional healers called *sangomas* are important to many South Africans. Most are women and are identified by their headdresses. They will often wear beads to cover their face. These traditional healers use a variety of natural medicines to cure illnesses.

Nuclear and extended family relationships are important to Afrikaners, as is the Church. Many young Afrikaners, part of the "born free" generation, feel conflicted. They live in a new more democratic world, yet they are still pulled by their Afrikaner heritage. As a result, there is a feeling of insecurity among many Afrikaner families. As with other segments of South African society, Afrikaner families have also had to deal with the political and social changes in a postapartheid world. The parents, grandparents, and great grandparents of Afrikaner adolescents and teens were responsible for apartheid, so in many ways, change has been a challenge for them. In

Zulu dancers entertaining spectators at the Ironman Triathlon in Port Elizabeth on the southern coast.

Desmond Mpilo Tutu is a social rights activist and retired Anglican bishop who stood against apartheid in the 1980s. He coined the term "rainbow nation" to describe the multiethnic society of post-apartheid South Africa.

the 1990s, many older Afrikaners left the country, refusing to participate in South African life. One sociologist generalized that many Afrikaner families have relatives living abroad.

In some families, parents send their children to so-called Afrikaner boot camps, where teens learn about their white heritage. Part of the reason these boot camps have become popular is that many Afrikaner teens cannot find jobs or believe they have been discriminated against because of their ethnicity. Still, many Afrikaners have embraced the new order and have found themselves in interracial social and business relationships. Indeed, many Afrikaner families have no problem socializing with blacks or Coloureds. In most nations, language unifies a people, but in South Africa the white minority used the Afrikaner language as a tool to control and separate. That has all changed in the postapartheid world, and today the country's myriad black languages are recognized as legal. South Africa's 4 million Coloured people speak Afrikaans, as do 3 million Afrikaners. South Africa is also home to about 1 million people of Asian descent, chiefly from India, Malaysia, and China. They speak a mixture of English, Asia languages, and Afrikaans.

Interpersonal relationships between South Africans of different races are still complicated, although legal barriers separating the two races have been torn down. Despite efforts to legislate equality, there are still major culture rifts in South African society, mostly because most whites are still wealthy while most blacks are still poor. As a result, bridging the racial divide is easier said than done. Four percent of marriages in South Africa are mixed (a large percentage considering South Africa's history, some experts say), although marriages between black and white seem to be the rarest. Black women are more likely to marry white men than black men are to marry white women. Most experts say this disparity is caused because black South African males tend to be poor, which forces some black women to seek financial security by marrying white men.

Nevertheless, people of different races now interact on a more personal level, especially when it comes to business. Many will socialize after work in restaurants. In business, they are more apt to build a long-term relationship. And the more educated a person is regardless of race, the more respected that person is by his or her peers. However, there are obstacles people must overcome. Some whites in South Africa, especially Afrikaners, continue to be paternalistic toward blacks.

VARYING OPINIONS ON RACE

According to the 2012 survey by the Institute for Justice and Reconciliation, 43.5 percent of South Africans rarely or never speak to a person of another race. Moreover, 27.4 percent say they always interact with a person of another race during weekdays, while 25.9 percent do so sometimes.

In a 2012 survey conducted by the Institute for Justice and Reconciliation, nearly 18 percent of those who responded said they often socialize with people of other races in their homes or in the homes of friends, while 21.6 percent socialize on occasion. Nearly 57 percent rarely or never socialize with a person of another race. Still, 18 percent of South Africans think it is wrong to live in an area in which half of their neighbors are of a different race. More than 20 percent said they would disapprove of working or taking orders from someone of a different race. While friendships and interpersonal relationships are often based on the color of a person's skin, economics also plays a role, and the differences between the poor and rich can be striking. These differences are played out every day when impoverished black maids clean the homes, cook the food, and rear the children of wealthy white employers.

Most domestic workers are uneducated black women, and the relationship between them and their white employers is seen by many as a microcosm of South African society. The domestics must make a grueling commute to work each day from their poor neighborhoods and pass through gated communities with expensive cars in the driveway.

This photo depicts an extended Coloured family who claim roots in Cape Town, Kimberley, and Pretoria.

The white families whose homes they clean are typically nuclear in their structure and wealthier than black, Coloured, Indian, or Asian households. The average size of a white household is 3.5 people.

FAMILY TIES

The extended family is just as important to South Africa's Coloureds and more traditional Afrikaan cultures as the nuclear family. However, English-speaking whites tend to focus more on the nuclear family.

Women in white households are still considered the traditional caretakers of children and the home, while men are the head of the household, the "breadwinners." White children have specific chores that they must do, regardless of their gender. And like children elsewhere, teenagers don't have a lot of pocket change and often ask their parents to spend money on what they might need.

Households headed by single women are on the upswing through all demographic groups in South Africa. About 14 percent of all households are now headed by women. In addition, men and women in the community are opting to live together outside of marriage.

In the 1990s, many white families left South Africa because they didn't want to deal with the political and social restructuring of the country. In recent years, however, many have returned, saying they have had a change of heart and want to help South Africa become more unified. According to some estimates, 340,000 have come back to the country.

TEXT-DEPENDENT QUESTIONS

1. Which areas did the Zulu migrate from?
2. Explain the differences between a nuclear family and an extended family.
3. In a patrilineal family, which person is the head of the household?

RESEARCH PROJECTS

1. Research the family practices and organization of a Native American group from your region. Write a brief report comparing those practices with those of the Zulu.
2. Create a family tree keeping in mind these questions: do you live in a nuclear family or an extended family? Is your family paternalistic, or is it maternalistic? What are the differences? Do you live in some other type of family? If so, research what that family unit is.

Citizens waiting in line to vote in the national general elections.

A traditional South African curry dish with dried apples, peppers, raisins, eggs, and rice.

WORDS TO UNDERSTAND

cuisine: a style of cooking.

encapsulate: to condense something.

indigenous: to be native born, or born of that country.

CHAPTER 3

Food and Drink

South African cuisine **encapsulates** the various influences that have infused South African society from its earliest days. From the native use of nuts, berries, and leaves to the **cuisine** of the Dutch, the Germans, the French, and the English, meat seems to be the only common thread connecting each cooking style.

The Dutch, the first to settle South Africa, brought with them most of the cooking methods South Africans use today. The Dutch liked to serve vegetables with butter and grated nutmeg, while cooking meat with herbs and spices such as hot pepper, cinnamon, nutmeg, and allspice. Dutch settlers brought not only their own recipes and cooking methods to South Africa, but the slaves of the Dutch East India Company provided what is perhaps the greatest contribution to the varied food tastes of South Africa.

When the Dutch arrived in South Africa, they brought with them many slaves from Southeast Asia. When these slaves arrived in South Africa, they continued to prepare food using their own cooking traditions. The result was the Cape Malay cuisine, a fusion of traditional South African fare, specifically from the country's west coast, and Malaysian cookery. In general, Cape Malay cuisine is a blend of strong flavors and a complex series of ingredients including fish, curries, cinnamon, saffron, and fruit. Breads, such as roti, which is a flatbread, and *sambals*, which are spicy sauces used to flavor many different dishes, are also staples of the Cape Malay food culture.

SOUTH AFRICAN STAPLES

Typical South African foods and dishes include *amasi,* a sour milk; bunny chow, a bread infused with curry; *blatjang*, a sweet sauce poured on meat; and *frikkadelle*, meatballs.

Bunny chow, a curry made of mutton, can be served in a bread bowl.

Bobotie is a spin on traditional shepherd's pie.

Over the centuries, Malay cooks improved many European dishes, including shepherd's pie. The Malay version of this all-meat-and-potato feast is *bobotie*. Malay cooks spiced up their meat pies with cumin, turmeric, coriander, allspice, and other spices. Instead of putting mashed potatoes on top of the pie as the Europeans did, Malay cooks topped their pie with a tasty egg custard.

The French, known throughout the world for their cuisine, added to the gastronomic tastes of South Africa as well. The Huguenots loved to use raisins in their dishes. They also grew grapes, which they turned into wine. The Germans brought with them their signature food, spicy sausage, which is now a common ingredient in many South African casseroles.

The French, German, and Dutch influence ultimately led to what chefs today call the Afrikaans style of cooking. The Afrikaners created recipes of dried meat, such as biltong, a type of beef jerky, which would last a long time without spoiling. They also used many spices and salts to preserve their fare. For their part, the British had a heavy hand in introducing roasted meats, roasted potatoes, and Yorkshire pudding as the preferred Sunday meal.

Despite these outside influences, South African food is still influenced by the traditional ingredients

Example of biltong.

used by the native populations. For centuries, these **indigenous** tribes lived off the produce they found or cultivated, which is why vegetables and meat are an important staple of the South African diet. Meat for stews and other dishes rarely came from the hunt, however, but were cultivated as livestock. Of course, Africa teems with wildlife and such animals as crocodile, ostrich, kudu (a kind of antelope), *mopane* worms, and warthog are often the main ingredients in many dishes.

Mopane worms are especially popular with the Venda people, a Bantu-speaking tribe that settled in the Soutpansberg, a mountain range in the northern part of the country. The Venda eat the caterpillar-like worms dried or cooked. These bugs are an important source of food in all of Africa. People dry and then grind the bugs into flour. Cooks will add the insects to spice up a stew or fry them as snacks. These crawlies are rich in iron.

The Zulus love grains and vegetables, including pumpkins, maize, and potatoes that they grow themselves. The Zulu drink curdled milk called *amazi,* which according to tradition can only be consumed by the person making it and their family members.

In addition to the Zulu, the Xhosa, who mainly live in the southeastern part of the country, are known for their meats, including goat. The Xhosa were

Pictured here is a dish of mealie pap with cabbage and vegetables.

A pot of *potjie* on an open fire.

Various meats grilling for *braai*, or barbecue.

herders. While they ate chickens and goats, they saved the sheep and cows for special occasions. At these events, the Xhosa slaughtered the animals as a token of appreciation to their ancestors.

While no one dish can be said to be truly South African, there are many traditional foods that continue to hold sway from one generation to the next. The most popular is mealie pap (pronounced "pup"), a corn flour porridge often served with meat and at breakfast. Mealie pap has been a staple of South Africa's poor black population for centuries. Many people eat the porridge every day. *Chakalaka*, a spicy dish made with mixed vegetables, oil, onion, chili pepper, beans, and other spices, is often served hot or cold with bread and mealie pap.

Everyone loves a barbeque, and South Africans are no exception. Cooking outdoors is popular because of the country's temperate climate. *Braai*, which means barbecue, is the traditional way of cooking meat over an open fire. Cooks can either grill meat over a flame or stew it over hot coals in a three-legged cast-iron pot called a *potjie*.

Although a person can *braai* just about any type of meat, including steak and lamb chops, a typical *braai* includes *boerewors*, a tasty sausage made with a variety of meats and spices. Like barbeques everywhere, the South African *braai*, which rhymes with "dry," is a popular way for friends and family to get together.

Before the Europeans arrived, beer was an important beverage for indigenous people. The Zulus, for example, brewed an alcoholic beer known as *utywala* and a nonalcoholic beer called *amahewu*. Traditional South African beer was so important to local societies that it became a focal point in many celebrations, especially weddings. Unlike European beer, the beer brewed in South Africa was low in alcohol and was mainly consumed as a health food because it was high in vitamins.

Milk from goats and cows is still an important part of the traditional black diet. Because there was no refrigeration in the rural areas, most varieties of milk are sour.

Not all cuisine in South Africa is traditional, nor does it revolve around the Dutch, German, French, or English. The Chinese, Italians, Japanese, Moroccans and West Africans, as well as American fast-food chains, have also influenced the South African diet.

Example of traditional *koeksisters*.

TEXT-DEPENDENT QUESTIONS

1. Explain how South African cuisine was influenced by immigrants from other countries and regions.

2. Why did the diet of the indigenous tribes revolve around nuts, berries, meat, and leaves?

3. How did the cultural traditions of South Africa impact the types of food that people eat?

RESEARCH PROJECTS

1. Research the traditional food of one of the Zulu groups in South Africa. Make a list of the kinds of food that are common alongside the types of nutrition—protein, carbohydrate, fat, vitamins, and minerals—the foods provide. In a brief paragraph, compare the list to what you eat and the kinds of nutrients you take in.

2. Go through your local phone book or an online directory and list the different types of restaurants in your area. Next, compare the types of food offered in these restaurants to the cultural and ethnic makeup of your community. What can you conclude?

Traditional Malay samosas filled with minced chicken and beef with lettuce.

Construction workers in Johannesburg, South Africa.

WORDS TO UNDERSTAND

acquiesced: agreed or complied with something in a reserved way.

integration: the process of opening up a place, community, or organization to all types of people.

precipitate: cause to start.

quintessential: like a perfect example of something.

sanction: a punishment imposed to force other governments to behave in a certain way.

CHAPTER 4

School, Work, and Industry

Erasmus Jacobs was the **quintessential** fifteen-year-old when he was playing on his father's farm on the south bank of the Orange River one day in March 1867. As he sat under the shade of an old tree, Erasmus noticed a shiny stone lying on the ground gleaming in the sunlight. Several weeks later, a neighbor, Schalk van Niekerk, noticed the glasslike stone that Erasmus and his sister were playing with and offered to buy it from them. The children's mother would hear nothing of the sort. She told van Niekerk that he could keep the stone.

The shiny object Van Niekerk left with was a diamond. Two years later diamonds were found in sufficient quantities to **precipitate** a "rush" of thousands of fortune hunters to the Orange and Vaal Rivers.

Cut and polished diamonds.　　　　　Stacked gold bars.

Diamonds, and later gold, changed the face of South Africa. The British quickly annexed the diamond fields, ignoring and later fighting the Dutch who lived there. Although the first mines were small, the British consolidated them to the point where the entire diamond industry was controlled by one monopolistic company, Cecil Rhode's De Beers Consolidated Mines.

DIAMOND IN THE ROUGH

Why are diamonds so rare? Diamonds form when the earth squeezes carbon deep below the ground under tremendous pressure. Eventually the pressure forces a few diamonds to the surface. In fact, only 350 tons (317,515 kg) of diamonds have been mined.

Diamonds and gold are today the most important segments of South Africa's economy. The nation is the richest country in the world in terms of mineral wealth, producing more than half of the world's supply of gold, its chief export.

South Africa's economy has been buoyed in recent years by globalization, as countries become more and more connected by transportation, communication, and other technologies. However, South Africa had to shed its apartheid policies before the international community fully embraced the country.

In fact, during the 1980s, international **sanctions** isolated South African firms from the global market. Those sanctions were lifted when apartheid ended. In a 1992 trip to an economic summit in Switzerland, Nelson Mandela, who was released from prison in 1990 and was looked upon as a leader by many inside and outside the country, proposed that for South Africa to grow economically, socially, and politically, its future had to be based on economic globalization. Mandela's view of an open globalized economy—which held sway after he was elected president in 1994—was met with some skepticism, but ultimately his critics **acquiesced**.

Today, foreign vehicle manufacturers such as BMW, Ford, Volkswagen, and Toyota, among others, have opened production plants, while many other companies have built factories that make automobile parts. Barclays, one of the largest banking companies in the world, acquired South Africa's largest consumer bank in 2005, while the Commercial Bank of China bought a stake in South Africa's largest financial services company. In 2011, the American retailer Walmart invested in the South African supermarket chain, Massmart.

Containers ready for shipment at the harbor entrance in Durban.

A lavender field in Paarl, in the southern part of the country.

Globalization helped turn South Africa into one of world's largest emerging economies, allowing it to take its place alongside Brazil, Russia, India, and China. Between 1990 and 2005, exports of manufactured goods from South Africa increased an average 6.7 percent a year. Moreover, South Africa began investing on the African continent itself, especially in the mining, agriculture, banking, financial services, retail merchandising, and telecommunication industries.

While industry greases South Africa's economy, nearly 14 percent of South Africans make their living as farmers. Mostly they grow corn, wheat, oats, sugarcane, and sunflowers, and they herd sheep and cattle. The wine industry in South Africa also has a worldwide reputation. However, most of South Africa's farmland is still owned by whites. Before apartheid, whites had simply thrown blacks off their land, a practice that continued during the apartheid years. After democracy came to South Africa in 1994, the government undertook a land redistribution program, which has placed a big financial burden on the government as it pays to settle land claims. So far, only 30 percent of the nations' farmland is open to blacks.

A CURE FOR SCURVY

Winemaking in South Africa dates all the way back to the earliest European exploration of the region. The first grapes were harvested for wine in 1659, just seven years after the Dutch East India Company arrived in Cape Town. The wine was intended to help ward off scurvy, a disease caused by Vitamin C deficiency, in its sailors.

Despite South Africa's economic success in the postapartheid world, many South Africans remain poor. Millions flock to the cities each year looking for work. While construction projects dot the skyline of these cities signifying that money is flowing into the country, it is still hard for many South Africans to find jobs.

Part of the reason is their lack of education. Although more black children now attend school than ever before, in the apartheid world of South Africa, education for nonwhites was inferior. The Bantu Education Act of 1953 widened the disparity. The architects of the law believed that blacks should only receive enough education for "certain forms of labor," insisting that educating blacks should not take away government resources meant for the education of whites. Although white, Coloured, and Asian children were required to attend school between the ages of seven and sixteen, the government said that black students had only to attend class between the ages of seven and eleven. Black children did not go to school to receive a good education but to prepare them for low-level, menial jobs. Compared to white schools, black schools had inferior facilities, teachers, and textbooks.

When democracy came, overhauling the school system was one of the government's prime responsibilities. Under the country's new constitution, everyone is guaranteed the right to a good education, which the government must provide. As a result, the government integrated all primary and secondary schools. The idea of one school for whites, the other for blacks, was abolished. A "No-Fee Schools" policy did away with school fees in the poorest primary schools, allowing more poor children to attend class.

A vineyard in the hills of Stellenbosch, in southern South Africa.

However, income disparity has replaced race as a segregating factor in South African schools. Generally, children from wealthy families receive a better education than children from poor families. Parents wealthy enough to send their children to private schools often do, and the competition is great. Private schools have better resources than the public schools and most are located in white communities. In 2013, 85 percent of private-school students had grades good enough to attend college.

That is not the case in public school. According to statistics provided by the government, 78 percent of South African public school students who took their high school certificate exams in 2013 passed. However, only 31 percent had grades good enough to get into a university. For those with low test marks, they have no other alternative except to learn a trade, go to a technical college, or enter the job market with diminished skills.

Students of the Percy Mdala High School, Knysna, South Africa , on the southern coast.

TEXT-DEPENDENT QUESTIONS

1. Explain the concept of globalization.

2. Explain why international sanctions would force South Africa to abandon the practice of apartheid.

3. Why would the government want to redistribute land and property?

RESEARCH PROJECTS

1. Research and write an essay about the environmental impact of gold mining.

2. Research and create a timeline of the gold and diamond industry in South Africa. Make sure your timeline has a brief description of each event.

Girls playing in a soccer match in Durban.

Ndebele women selling traditional dolls.

WORDS TO UNDERSTAND

concertina: a small accordion with buttons.

defining: important; distinctive; essential for something's identity.

legislation: the process of writing and passing laws.

provincial: belonging to a province or region outside of the
main cities of a country.

CHAPTER 5

Arts and Entertainment

Nelsen Mandela had been president of South Africa for about a year when he trotted out onto the lush rugby field in the city of Johannesburg a bright winter's day in 1995. His presence elicited a symphony of cheers from the mostly black crowd: "Nelson! Nelson! Nelson!" they shouted with hearty voices.

Mandela, like most black South Africans, did not particularly like rugby. He preferred soccer. For Mandela and other blacks, rugby was a sport of the white elite, which they played with religious-like zeal. Still, Mandela came onto the field with a huge smile etched on his face. Clad in a green cap and a green long-sleeve rugby jersey, the colors of South Africa's national rugby team, the Springboks, the president shook the hands of the players who had just won the title game of the Rugby World Cup.

It was a **defining** moment in postapart-heid South Africa. The Springboks were racially segregated, beloved by whites and reviled by blacks. Yet, Mandela, wearing the number 6 on his back—the same number as the team's coach, Francois Pienaar—was acutely aware of the significance of the moment. Mandela hoped that one simple handshake, one simple rugby match could do what no law or **legislation** could do: bridge the wide divide that separated the nation. The symbolism was lost to no one.

South Africa (in green) playing against England in the final of the Rugby World Cup in 2007; its win that year gave South Africa its second world title.

A SIMPLE RUGBY MATCH

"Sport has the power to change the world," Mandela said after his symbolic appearance at the national rugby match in 1995. "It has the power to inspire, it has the power to unite people in a way that little else does."

Indeed, sports play a huge role in the lives of many South Africans. Perhaps it is because of the country's favorable climate, or the generous government funding that has resulted in the building of many sports parks and stadiums in communities that never had such facilities before. Or, perhaps, it is the world-class athletes, from runners to soccer players, that the nation produces. Whatever the reason, playing or watching sports is the top pastime of many South Africans, black and white, old and young.

Although South Africans play rugby at all levels—in schools, regional clubs, and on national teams—soccer is king, with the most popular clubs attract-ing the most fans. South Africa's national soccer team, the Bafana Bafana, is ranked in the Top 40 of all soccer teams in the world. It reached the World Cup Finals for the first time in 1998, after returning to international competition six years earlier. The international community banned the team from playing because of South Africa's apartheid policies.

In 1991, as apartheid was in its death throes, the International Olympic Committee allowed South Africa to complete in the 1992 Summer Olympics in Barcelona, Spain. However, it was not enough time for the South Africans to put together a multiethnic, multiracial team. Instead, the 120 athletes were mostly white. At the time, blacks had little access to training facilities and parks under apartheid and could not prepare themselves. In 2004, South African won six medals at the Summer Olympic Games in Athens, Greece. In 2010, South Africa hosted the World Cup, the most important soccer tournament in the world. The best players from around the globe descended on this once segregated society for several weeks of soccer and fun.

South Africa has always had a great cricket team. Basically a British game, it is played during the summer with a bat and ball. Thousands of spectators come to the games to see their favorite local club or **provincial** or national teams.

A NATIONAL NOVEL

South Africa's most famous novel is Alan Paton's *Cry, The Beloved Country*. Born in South Africa in 1903, Paton taught in South Africa's elite white schools. He later took a job in a prison for black youths. In 1948, he wrote the novel, which shines a light on racism but also offers hope as key characters overcome fears and hatreds.

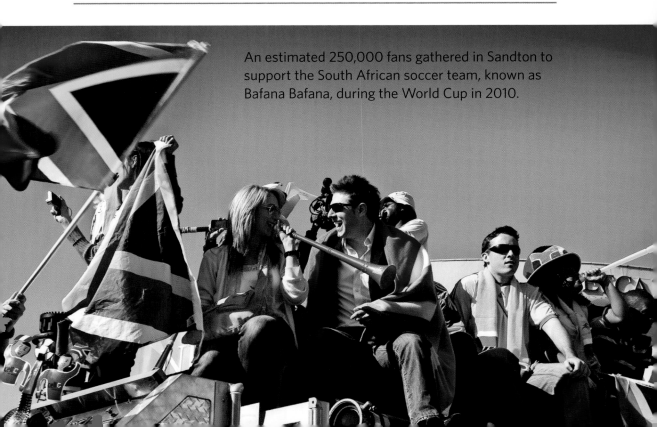

An estimated 250,000 fans gathered in Sandton to support the South African soccer team, known as Bafana Bafana, during the World Cup in 2010.

Drummers play before the start of the Nelson Mandela Bay Ironman Triathlon in 2009.

Just as South Africans love sports, they adore all kinds of music. Music in South Africa is a melting pot of different styles and rhythms, from Dutch folk music to hip-hop, to the strains of traditional African instruments. As the Boers journeyed northward on their Great Trek, they often sang religious songs and played such instruments as the violin and **concertina**. Eventually these sounds and songs developed in a traditional form of Afrikaner music called *boeremusiek*.

Choral singing, which began in South African churches, is now a competitive sport, where some of the best voices in the nation compete for top honors at choir festivals. One of the most popular vocal groups is Ladysmith Black Mambazo.

Music and dance have always played an important role in African culture, which is why both are very important to the Zulu, the largest ethnic group in South Africa. In Zulu society, songs and dances are passed from generation to generation. Music is important in everyday life, as well as for religious rites and ceremonies. Drumming is among the most popular African music traditions. The *djembe*, a drum carved out of a hollowed tree and covered in goatskin, is the best-known African drum played in South Africa, where it is also commercially produced.

Dancing and music is a group activity and symbolizes important events that are happening within a clan. The Zulus dance, with shakers and ankle bracelets, at important events including weddings and the birth of a child. Dances are a sign of happiness and take on various forms. The bull dance, for example, originated in the dormitories where male Zulu miners worked. The dance imitates a bull. During the hunting dance, the Zulus mimic hunters on the prowl. They wave sticks representing the spears hunters use. Females participate in their own version of the dance as they "welcome" the men back from the hunt.

South Africa's Coloured population, descended from the intermarriage of white settlers, native Africans, and Asian slaves, takes to the streets of Cape

The prison, and now museum, on Robben Island where Nelson Mandela remained for eighteen years.

MAXIMUM
SECURITY
PRISON

In July 2014, seventy-five groups comprised of 40,000 minstrels participated in the annual Tweede Nuwe Jaar Parade.

Town each new year to celebrate the Coloureds' Carnival. The carnival is a vibrant scene, with umbrellas of different hues and painted faces. Various bands, troupes, singers, and choirs march down Cape Town's streets, celebrating life, music, and an annual rite of renewal.

The parade harkens back to the 1800s when ships from the United States docked at Cape Town. The locals listened and imitated the music the sailors brought with them. Most of the musical groups that participate in the carnival come from the poor, working-class neighborhoods in and around Cape Town. During the apartheid years, the government banned the Coloureds from parading in the streets. The celebration had to be held in a stadium. When democracy came to South Africa, the carnival once again took to the boulevards.

TEXT-DEPENDENT QUESTIONS

1. When did South Africa host the soccer's World Cup?

2. Why do you think traditional African music and dance are important to the culture of South Africa?

3. What is it about South Africa's past that provides a treasure trove of material for writers?

RESEARCH PROJECTS

1. Museums, such as the District Six Museum, often compile oral histories of people who live through a specific historic event. Find a person, such as a grandparent, uncle, friend, or teacher, who has lived through a historic event and interview them about that moment in history. Record the interview using a voice recorder or digital camera. You can also take notes. Before the interview, research the event and then write down a list of questions you want to ask. When you are finished, you can write up the interview in a question-and-answer format or publish the audio and video online.

2. Research Ladysmith Black Mambazo and another popular South African vocal group on the Internet. Listen to two to three of each of the group's songs and list the qualities of each in two columns. Write a short paragraph about the similarities and difference between the groups.

A traditionally painted hut of the Ndebele tribe.

The famous houses of Donkin Street in Port Elizabeth in the Eastern Cape Province.

WORDS TO UNDERSTAND

consortium: organizations or groups that band together for a common purpose.

savanna: grassy plains dotted with trees in a tropical or subtropical region.

subtropical: relating to areas between tropical and temperate regions where conditions are nearly always tropical, that is, hot and humid.

CHAPTER 6

Cities, Towns, and the Countryside

From its craggy coastlines to its vibrant cities to the verdant forests that teem with a dazzling array of plants and animals, South Africa is a traveler's dream, the entire world wrapped in one country. From city to village, coastline to mountain and back again, South Africa is a landscape of contrasts. Parts of the country receive little rainfall, while other areas are wet. The country's mountains run north to south, marching up to the coast. The gleaming cityscapes of Cape Town and Johannesburg are inundated with slums. In the countryside, poor villages have no electricity, running water, or health facilities.

The most beautiful city is arguably Cape Town, which is framed by the glistening blue waters of the Atlantic Ocean to its south and the Table Mountain

Aerial view of Cape Town showing Table Mountain and the Cape Town Harbour.

to its north. As the second most populous city in South Africa, Cape Town is South Africa's heart and soul, the first place the Dutch staked out as their own. Visitors can see the Company's Garden, established in the 1650s by the first settlers. The garden is today a public park, where roses, a fishpond, and aviary greet the curious. Inside the garden, located in the center of the city, are more than 8,000 species of plants.

THE KRUGER NATIONAL PARK

Much of South Africa is still an untamed wilderness, and no area exemplifies this more than the Kruger National Park, the largest game reserve in the country and one of the largest wildlife sanctuaries in the world. The park is as large as Israel and teems with wildlife, including elephants and cheetahs.

Durban is South Africa's largest port and its third largest city. With its **subtropical** climate, the city can be unbearably hot in the summer. The city is home to more than 33,000 people of Indian descent. Like many other cities, Durban was once off limits to blacks, but today the Zulus have made their homes in the city's central district. Both the Indians and Zulus now outnumber whites who once dominated the town.

Johannesburg's skyline is modern, with skyscrapers and apartment buildings towering over the city center. Nearly 6 million people live in the country's most populous city, including 2 million people who live in Soweto, South Africa's largest black township. The suburbs around the city once housed only whites, but today many middle-class blacks live in these once-exclusive enclaves.

During the apartheid years, the government built small shacks for blacks, calling them "matchbox houses" because each was shaped like a square. Violence bloomed, and anger brewed. Today, more than twenty years after the election of Nelson Mandela, the slums of South Africa are not much better. Murders, rapes, and other crimes occur every day. Many people live in squalor, with no running water, sewage treatment, or electricity. As a result, more and more people are moving to the inner city, where life is not much better. Away from the clean streets that only tourists see, South Africa's cities overflow with poverty as people build shacks on any open land they can find.

NAME CHANGING

South Africa is always a nation in transition. After full democracy was established in 1994, the government began changing the names of streets, airports, and other locations as it moved away from apartheid. Johannesburg's International Airport is now Tambo Airport. For many years, people have wanted to change Pretoria to Tshwane, which they have yet to do.

Even the coastline of South Africa is a study in contrast, where winds, mountains, and ocean currents determine the climate. The tropical Agulhas

An elephant in the Kruger National Park, in the northeastern part of the country.

Current flows south down the east coast, which is lined with rich and fertile forests. The west coast is arid as the colder Benguela Current flows northward. The two currents slam into one another at Cape Agulhas, the southernmost point of the African continent.

Because of these oddities of nature, the plants and animals living along both coasts are varied. For example, along the west coast the temperature of the water averages only 57 degrees Fahrenheit, producing little precipitation. Many saltwater-loving creatures, such as the sea anemone, thrive here and elsewhere. On the east coast, conditions are hot and humid. Many types of plants and animals, including coral reefs and exotic flowers, live in this sub-tropical environment.

The ocean in the southernmost coast also provides major waves for adventurous surfers from across the globe. The waves are so gnarly that the 2014 World Surfing Games were held off Cape Town. The bays and points around the coastline make for some radical swells—just watch out for sharks, the experts warn. Surfers see the best waves from March to September.

One of South Africa's emerging businesses is cultural tourism, where visitors can travel deep into the country to see how the indigenous population lives. Africans from the Pedi, Zulu, Xhosa, and Basotho tribes, among others, spend their days tending cattle, molding clay pots, weaving baskets, and taking part in ritual dances.

When Nelson Mandela died in 2013, he was buried in his ancestral home in Qunu. Mandela wrote the following in his autobiography:

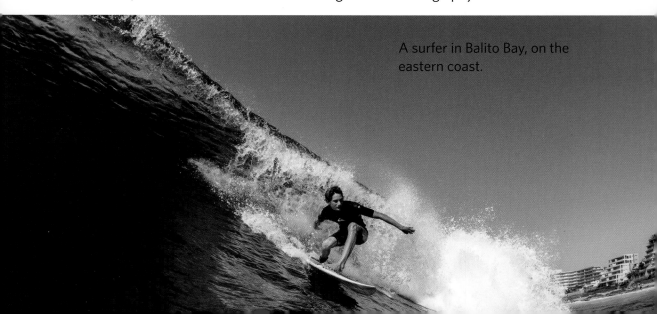

A surfer in Balito Bay, on the eastern coast.

A Basotho hut in the east, in Golden Gate Highlands National Park.

Nature was our playground. The hills above Qunu were dotted with large smooth rocks which we transformed into our own rollercoaster. We sat on flat stones and slid down the face of the rocks. We did this until our backsides were so sore we could hardly sit down.

Although he was born in the nearby village of Mvezo, Qunu was always Mandela's home. Not much has changed in the town. The region is remote and poor, although there is a hospital named for the president.

Some of the cone-shaped thatched-roof huts of mud that dotted the town when Mandela was a child have been replaced with simple and poor matchbox houses. The gum trees where Mandela learned history are sprinkled across the landscape. Children pour drinking water into large containers at their schools. Boys still herd sheep, walking with them down village roads.

Across South Africa, many rural villages lack the basic amenities that the tourists have come to expect in their own lives, including clean water, hospitals, and electricity. Many of the rural poor must walk two hours each way to find water, which is often fetid and unhealthy. However, things are slowly changing. In 1997, South Africa's national and local governments in the Eastern Cape began a partnership with the World Bank and a French water-management company to bring clean water to a quarter of the population that lacked clean water.

They called the effort Amanz Abantu, which in the Xhosa language means "water for the people." In the village of Cisira, for example, the **consortium** laid water pipes from a nearby river and built a filtering station to cleanse the water before people drank it. Today, millions of people have clean drinking water.

Although South Africa is the continent's most modern country, an estimated 3 million do not have electricity. Among those were the residents of Gwakwani, a remote village in the north. In the Venda language the village's name means "armpit." In 2014, this dot on the map became electrified, something villagers have always wanted. The energy came from solar panels installed by engineers from the University of Johannesburg.

It wasn't that long ago that South Africa overflowed with wildlife. Elephants, hyenas, leopards, lions, giraffes, and other species marched the across the **savanna** where blonde grass waved in the wind. As the country's population grew and humans needed more space to live, they pushed many species to the point of extinction. Today, many species are protected, living in game preserves. In fact, farmers who live in traditional wildlife areas in the eastern part of the country have stopped farming and herding. They now make a living by running private game preserves.

Giraffes walking in the savanna.

TEXT-DEPENDENT QUESTIONS

1. Describe the living conditions in the townships and slums of South Africa.

2. What is the least expensive way to get energy to remote villages?

3. Why would people go to great lengths to find clean water?

RESEARCH PROJECTS

1. Research the Linnaeus system of classifying plants. Pick one species of plant in South Africa and classify it by kingdom, phylum, class, order, family, genus, and species. Next, devise your own classification system for a few objects in the classroom. Using the Linnaeus system as a model, develop at least four levels of classification. Start out with one classification level that divides all the objects in the room into two major categories, such as "natural" and "artificial."

2. Research the Kruger National Park and create a travel guide for a photographic safari tourists might want to take. In your guide, you can talk about the park's animals, landscape, and other features. Create an itinerary of the safari.

The Blyde River Canyon, in the northeast province of Mpumalanga.

FURTHER RESEARCH

Online

The Central Intelligence Agency's World Fact Book on South Africa provides up-to-date statistics, a short history, and maps: https://www.cia.gov/library/publications/the-world-factbook/geos/sf.html.

Find South Africa's official government website here: http://www.gov.za.

Learn more about tourism in South Africa by visiting http://www.southafrica.net/country/us/en and http://www.southafrica.com.

Learn more about famous South African food by visiting http://www.hillmanwonders.com/cuisines/south_africa_top_10_spec.htm.

Find out more about South African cultures and languages by visiting http://www.sa-venues.com/sa_languages_and_culture.htm.

Books

Crais, Clifton. *The South Africa Reader: History, Culture, Politics.* Durham, NC: Duke University Press, 2013.

Holmes, Anthony. *South Africa: History in an Hour.* New York: HarperPress, 2012.

Holt-Biddle, David. *South Africa—Culture Smart!* London: Kuperard, 2007.

National Geographic. *National Geographic Traveler: South Africa.* 2ND ED. Des Moines: National Geographic Books, 2013.

Thompson, Leonard. *A History of South Africa.* 4TH ED. New Haven, CT: Yale University Press, 2014.

Wilsen, Aileen. *South African Cooking in the USA.* Cape Point: Cape Point Press, 2010.

NOTE TO EDUCATORS: This book contains both imperial and metric measurements as well as references to global practices and trends in an effort to encourage the student to gain a worldly perspective. We, as publishers, feel it's our role to give young adults the tools they need to thrive in a global society.

SERIES GLOSSARY

ancestral: relating to ancestors, or relatives who have lived in the past.

archaeologist: a scientist that investigates past societies by digging in the earth to examine their remains.

artisanal: describing something produced on a small scale, usually handmade by skilled craftspeople.

colony: a settlement in another country or place that is controlled by a "home" country.

commonwealth: an association of sovereign nations unified by common cultural, political, and economic interests and traits.

communism: a social and economic philosophy characterized by a classless society and the absence of private property.

continent: any of the seven large land masses that constitute most of the dry land on the surface of the earth.

cosmopolitan: worldly; showing the influence of many cultures.

culinary: relating to the kitchen, cookery, and style of eating.

cultivated: planted and harvested for food, as opposed to the growth of plants in the wild.

currency: a system of money.

demographics: the study of population trends.

denomination: a religious grouping within a faith that has its own organization.

dynasty: a ruling family that extends across generations, usually in an autocratic form of government, such as a monarchy.

ecosystems: environments where interdependent organisms live.

endemic: native, or not introduced, to a particular region, and not naturally found in other areas.

exile: absence from one's country or home, usually enforced by a government for political or religious reasons.

feudal: a system of economic, political, or social organization in which poor landholders are subservient to wealthy landlords; used mostly in relation to the Middle Ages.

globalization: the processes relating to increasing international exchange that have resulted in faster, easier connections across the world.

gross national product: the measure of all the products and services a country produces in a year.

heritage: tradition and history.

homogenization: the process of blending elements together, sometimes resulting in a less interesting mixture.

iconic: relating to something that has become an emblem or symbol.

idiom: the language particular to a community or class; usually refers to regular, "everyday" speech.

immigrants: people who move to and settle in a new country.

indigenous: originating in and naturally from a particular region or country.

industrialization: the process by which a country changes from a farming society to one that is based on industry and manufacturing.

SERIES GLOSSARY

integration: the process of opening up a place, community, or organization to all types of people.

kinship: web of social relationships that have a common origin derived from ancestors and family.

literacy rate: the percentage of people who can read and write.

matriarchal: of or relating to female leadership within a particular group or system.

migrant: a person who moves from one place to another, usually for reasons of employment or economic improvement.

militarized: warlike or military in character and thought.

missionary: one who goes on a journey to spread a religion.

monopoly: a situation where one company or state controls the market for an industry or product.

natural resources: naturally occurring materials, such as oil, coal, and gold, that can be used by people.

nomadic: describing a way of life in which people move, usually seasonally, from place to place in search of food, water, and pastureland.

nomadic: relating to people who have no fixed residence and move from place to place.

parliament: a body of government responsible for enacting laws.

patriarchal: of or relating to male leadership within a particular group or system.

patrilineal: relating to the relationship based on the father or the descendants through the male line.

polygamy: the practice of having more than one spouse.

provincial: belonging to a province or region outside of the main cities of a country.

racism: prejudice or animosity against people belonging to other races.

ritualize: to mark or perform with specific behaviors or observances.

sector: part or aspect of something, especially of a country's or region's economy.

secular: relating to worldly concerns; not religious.

societal: relating to the order, structure, or functioning of society or community.

socioeconomic: relating to social and economic factors, such as education and income, often used when discussing how classes, or levels of society, are formed.

statecraft: the ideas about and methods of running a government.

traditional: relating to something that is based on old historical ways of doing things.

urban sprawl: the uncontrolled expansion of urban areas away from the center of the city into remote, outlying areas.

urbanization: the increasing movement of people from rural areas to cities, usually in search of economic improvement, and the conditions resulting this migration.

INDEX

Italicized page numbers refer to illustrations.

INDEX

INDEX

INDEX

PHOTO CREDITS

Page	Page Location	Archive/Photographer	Page	Page Location	Archive/Photographer
6	Full page	Dreamstime/Photosimo	30	Bottom right	Dreamstime/Micoppiens
8	Top	iStock.com/ruvanboshoff	31	Bottom	Dreamstime/Anke Van Wyk
10	Top left	Wikimedia Commons/Paul Weinberg	32	Top	Dreamstime/Alan Gignoux
10	Bottom	Dreamstime/Antonella865	34	Top left	Dreamstime/Sebastian Kaulitzki
11	Top left	Wikimedia Commons/Charles Davidson Bell	34	Top right	Dreamstime/Atu Studio Atu Studio
12	Top	Wikimedia Commons/Charles Davidson Bell	35	Bottom	Dreamstime/Lcswart
			36	Top right	Dreamstime/Daleen Loest
13	Top right	Dreamstime/Yulan	37	Bottom	Dreamstime/Peter Wollinga
14	Top	Wikimedia Commons/rahuldlucca	38	Bottom	Dreamstime/Gabriel Robledo
15	Bottom	Dreamstime/Neal Cooper	39	Bottom	Dreamstime/Chris Van Lennep
16	Top	Dreamstime/Alan Gignoux	40	Top	Dreamstime/Inna Felker
18	Top	Dreamstime/Temistocle Lucarelli	42	Top right	Dreamstime/ Grosremy
19	Bottom left	Dreamstime/Anke Van Wyk	43	Bottom	Dreamstime/Patrick Allen
20	Top left	Wikimedia Commons/Benny Gool	44	Top	Dreamstime/Michael Sheehan
22	Top left	Wikimedia Commons/Henry M. Trotter	45	Bottom	Dreamstime/Superbbs
23	Bottom	Dreamstime/Anke Van Wyk	46	Top	Dreamstime/Wesley Klue
24	Top	Dreamstime/Micoppiens	47	Bottom	Dreamstime/Daleen Loest
26	Bottom	Dreamstime/Paul Brighton	48	Top	Dreamstime/Anke Van Wyk
27	Top	Dreamstime/Micoppiens	50	Top	Dreamstime/Andrea Willmore
27	Bottom right	Dollar Photo Club/Tinus Potgieter	51	Bottom	Dreamstime/Kaye Eileen Oberstar
28	Bottom left	Wikimedia Commons/Mark Skipper	52	Bottom	Dreamstime/Chris Van Lennep
29	Top left	Dreamstime/Fultonsphoto	53	Top	Dreamstime/Brad White
29	Top right	Dreamstime/Anke Van Wyk	54	Bottom	Dreamstime/Jan Martin Will
			55	Bottom	Dreamstime/Demerzel21

COVER

Top	Dollar Photo Club/michaeljung
Bottom left	Dollar Photo Club/Instinia
Bottom right	Dollar Photo Club/Dmitry Ersler

ABOUT THE AUTHOR

John Perritano is an award-winning journalist, writer, and editor from Southbury, Connecticut, who has written numerous articles and books on history, culture, and science for publishers that include National Geographic's *Reading Expedition Series* and its *Global Issues Series*, focusing on such topics as globalization, population, and natural resources. He has also been a contributor to Discovery.com, *Popular Mechanics*, and other magazines and websites. He holds a master's degree in American History from Western Connecticut State University.